11 Days After 9/11

Vanessa R. Pittman

13TH & JOAN

For permission requests, write to the publisher, addressed "Attention: Permissions Coordinator," 205 N. Michigan Avenue, Suite #810, Chicago, IL 60601. 13th & Joan books may be purchased for educational, business or sales promotional use. For information, please email the Sales Department at sales@13thandjoan.com.

Printed in the U. S. A.

First Printing, September 2024.

Library of Congress Cataloging-in-Publication Data has been applied for.

ISBN: 978-1-961863-97-2

I dedicate this book to all the heroes and families of the NYPD, FDNY, NY/NJ Port Authority Police, Triborough Bridge and Tunnel Police, volunteers from all over the world, MTA Police, U.S. Military (Army, Navy, Marines, Coast Guard, Air Force, National Guard), and the 9/11 victims of the Twin Towers, the Pentagon, Flight 11, Flight 175 and Flight 93. In addition, I want to remember the victims of the World Trade Center Bombing of 1993. Also, I especially dedicate this book to those who lived, worked and/or attended school in the area of Ground Zero and still passing away from illnesses tied to the 9/11 attacks. I continually pray for my fellow 9/11 survivors. We all live with the knowledge that long life is not promised to us, but vow to live our lives to the fullest not just for ourselves, but for our families as well. God Bless You!

Adversity is the vessel in which the soul is tempered,
revealing the strength we never knew we possessed
and the wisdom that only the harshest trials can bestow.

Contents

Acknowledgements

As I sit down to pen the words that will introduce my first of many books to the world, I find myself overwhelmed with gratitude for the unwavering support of my family. They say that behind every great achievement lies a network of loving hearts and in my case, this sentiment couldn't be truer.

To my mother Geraldine, whose boundless love and encouragement have been the guiding force behind every step of my journey, I owe the deepest of gratitude. Your belief in me, even during times of uncertainty, has been my rock, propelling me forward when doubts threatened to cloud my path. Thank you for instilling in me the values of perseverance, compassion, and resilience, virtues that I hold dear and that have shaped the very essence of this book.

To my children, Taèlor and DeAndré, whose laughter and camaraderie have filled my life with joy and inspiration, thank you for being my constant companions in both the highs and lows of life. Your unwavering support and understanding have been a source of strength, reminding me that no dream is too big when pursued with passion and determination.

To Andraea Chanel my bonus daughter, I'm proud you welcomed me into your life.

During this time, I have to also acknowledge the entire Staff of the Police Commissioner's Office, in particular Police Commissioners Raymond W. Kelly, Bernard Kerik and Deputy Commissioner Michael J. Farrell.

To my extended family—aka my girl crew from the New York City Police Department, aka NYPD and DOE—Kai, Jovona, Tracey, Marie, Kristel, Ajuba, Debra, Monique, Kathleen, Yvonne, Jessica Tisch, Lauralee, Lisa, and Nancy, whose love knows no bounds, thank you for your unyielding encouragement and belief in my potential. Your words of wisdom and encouragement have served as a guiding light, illuminating my path even in the darkest of times.

To the Davis Family, especially my Sister In Christ, Yolanda, thank you for being you.

And last but not least, the Howell/Spencer, Pittman/Johnson families and the love of my life, André. This book is as much yours as it is mine. It is a testament to the power of familial love and support, without which this journey would have been infinitely more challenging. As you embark on this literary adventure with me, know that each page is imbued with the spirit of gratitude and love that I hold for each and every one of you.

With heartfelt thanks,
Vanessa

Introduction

September 11, 2001, marked the beginning of a journey that would forever alter the trajectory of my life. Although millions of others around the world watched in horror as the events of that fateful day unfolded on television screens, I actually witnessed it first-hand as a civilian member of the New York City Police Department Office of the Police Commissioner. The images were seared into my memory with an intensity that defies description and will live with me for the rest of my life.

Little did I know then that I would soon become intimately acquainted with the profound and lasting impact of those events. As a survivor of 9/11, I found myself thrust into a reality defined by loss, trauma, and uncertainty—a reality that would shape my identity in ways I could never have imagined.

This book is my attempt to make sense of that reality, to navigate the complexities of survivorship, and to give voice to the myriad emotions and experiences that have colored my journey over the past 23 years. It is a story of resilience in the face of adversity, of finding hope and purpose amidst the wreckage of tragedy, and of learning to embrace life anew in the aftermath of unspeakable loss.

But it is also a story of community and connection, of the count-less individuals who rallied around me in my darkest hours, offering support, solace, and a reminder that I was not alone in my struggle. It is a testament to the power of human compassion and solidarity and to the healing that can emerge from shared experiences of pain and trauma.

As I invite you into the intimate corners of my heart and mind, I do so with humility and vulnerability, knowing that the journey ahead is not an easy one. Yet it is a journey that I undertake with courage and conviction, guided by a belief in the resilience of the human spirit and the transformative power of storytelling.

May my words serve as a beacon of hope for fellow survivors, a source of understanding for those who seek to comprehend the complexities of our experiences, and a tribute to the enduring spirit of resilience that binds us together as survivors of 9/11.

Psalm 91:1-2 *He that dwelleth in the secret place of the most High shall abide under the shadow of the Almighty. I will say of the LORD, He is my refuge and my fortress: my God; in him will I trust.*

Pillar 1

$\mathcal{S}$ometimes, things change in an instant in ways that demand the best from us. Sometimes, we didn't know there was better in us to give. How would you respond to being needed in the midst of chaos?

MY STORY

My whole life changed in a single moment. I couldn't have imagined what was going to happen or what my life would become after the events of that day. No one will ever forget.

On the day of Tuesday, September 11, 2001, it was...*different*. It was beautiful outside and there wasn't a cloud in the sky. It was primary election day, and everyone was going to go and vote. I was running late for work and couldn't be bothered to think about voting without first satisfying my hunger, so I looked to my belly and said, "You know what I want for food."

I was pregnant and I was having an intense craving. I was the type of pregnant person who wanted what she wanted when she wanted it. And if I didn't get it, I was going to be a mad person. That day, my baby and I wanted Krispy Kreme, and the nearest location was at the World Trade Center. Something in me said that the day wasn't starting like any other day, so I didn't get the donut and rushed into the office to get to my desk as close to 8:30 as possible instead. Cravings would have to wait and besides, I could grab a bagel and tea on the way.

I worked as an executive assistant at police headquarters back then and that morning, my desk resembled the construction zone our office was in. There was a lot of work piled on top of it. I heard what I thought was the sound of construction debris being tossed off the 15-story rooftop above me on the 14th floor. It was a normal thing to hear while our portion of the building was being upgraded, but someone yelling from across the office wasn't.

"Oh my gosh! Something hit the Trade Center," they screamed to everyone in the room.

No one could have ever thought that the "something" would have been an entire airplane. The North Tower was hit at 8:46 a.m. that day. It was only 16 minutes into my workday. By the time we realized what was truly going on, chaos ensued.

Everyone was going crazy because you could see the plane partially sticking out of the building. They were both on fire. When I looked back down in front of my desk, one of the police commissioner's bodyguards was standing in front of me. The only thing I could think to do was ask how I could help. I accepted an order to relay some important information across the department before I turned my attention to my personal life.

I called my then boyfriend André to make sure he wasn't nearby. I was worried because he sometimes delivered freight in the area. I called my mom and told her a plane hit the building, but that was all I knew at the time.

When the second plane hit the South Tower at 9:03 a.m., I was on the phone with a friend. That's when we got the call to evacuate. As a typical New Yorker, I commuted to and from work in sneakers and changed into my heels in the office every day. I didn't even have time to change back into my sneakers. Nothing mattered beyond my bag, wallet, key, and safety. I wasn't entirely aware of everything happening around me, but a detective escorted me out of the building because we were no longer taking the elevators.

She guided me down the 14 floors, through the chaos and fear. Once we were outside, the scene was completely crazy. There were police everywhere and sirens could be heard from every direction as more came to help. An announcement on a speaker directed all civilian members of the police force to immediately go home.

I drifted into a crowd of strangers and coworkers as we made our way through Chinatown to the Brooklyn Bridge. If you watch old footage of that day now, you see how the entire street was covered in smoke and dust. In the moment, I wasn't aware of any of it. I only knew that a bridge was the last place I wanted to be after an attack without warning on the World Trade Center.

I remember telling my coworkers, "We are on a bridge and you don't know what the next target is. I am not trying to be on a bridge."

That's when I became aware of the dust.

I'd made it to the Brooklyn side of the bridge from Manhattan where there were buses waiting to shuttle people away from the scene. Looking out of the bus window, I saw all these people covered in dust. I remember seeing a dust-covered Muslim woman crying. A Black man who was covered in just as much debris was yelling at her, telling her that "her people" had done this.

And that's when I learned that both towers had collapsed.

I was surrounded by anger, tears, fear, confusion, and hatred. I was just trying to get home as soon and as safely as possible.

I can't begin to describe the relief I felt when I made it to my destination in Starrett City, Brooklyn, more than four hours later, and saw my boyfriend waiting at home for me. He'd gone to work that day, but not in Manhattan. We learned that the planes hitting the towers was no accident. They were acts of terror. The first thing I wanted to do was get my daughter from daycare.

My boyfriend tried to convince me to wait a while for traffic to break up, but I had no interest in waiting. I didn't want to sit down and rest. I didn't want to change my clothes. I didn't even want to talk to anybody. I just wanted to get my child. She hadn't even had her first birthday yet and I needed to hug her.

When I finally got to the daycare, she was running around like she always did. She saw me and she squealed with delight. That moment was the best moment I felt the entire, horrific day. She was so happy to see me and I grabbed her not realizing that I had dust on me. I was around so many people who had all that dust on them, not knowing that I had it on me, too. It didn't matter to me. I just hugged her and I kept hugging her. The stress melted away.

MY LESSON

Looking back, had I been stubborn and gone to Krispy Kreme, I could have lost not only my life but my unborn son as well.

People left for work that morning, never to be with their families again. Once I processed that and saw the footage on TV, I was dumbfounded. From that point forward, my life totally changed.

Don't take any day or life for granted. Period. It's a blessing to leave your house and return back to it.

THE BLESSING

The events surrounding 9/11 gifted me with an awareness and a deep sense of gratitude that I didn't have before. I've always loved God, my family, and my community, but something in me changed the moment I nearly lost my connection to them all. We lost a lot that day, but my son was able to be born shortly after. My faith was renewed and deepened in ways I couldn't have known to ask God for.

THE AFFIRMATION

I am grateful for each day that God guides and protects me through.

REFLECTION QUESTIONS

1. Do you remember 9/11?

_____

_____

_____

2. Where were you on 9/11?

_____

_____

_____

3. Have you ever had something strange happen on a day when you went against your typical morning routine?

_____

_____

_____

4. Has life ever been challenging for you?

_____

_____

_____

5. Have you been through something traumatic in life?

_____

_____

_____

6. If so, what did you learn? If not, what do you think is an important lesson to take away from any traumatic event?

_____

_____

_____

7. Do you have a support system?

_____

_____

_____

8. Who is the first person you want to see when something goes
bad in your life?

_____

_____

_____

9. Do you have a family?

_____

_____

_____

10. Do you personally have to experience something traumatic to understand someone else's struggle?

_____

_____

_____

11. Would you stay or leave work if you witnessed something similar to 9/11?

_____

_____

_____

Psalm 23:1-6 *The Lord is my shepherd; I shall not want. He maketh me to lie down in green pastures: he leadeth me beside the still waters. He restoreth my soul: he leadeth me in the paths of righteousness for his name's sake. Yea, though I walk through the valley of the shadow of death, I will fear no evil: for thou art with me; thy rod and thy staff they comfort me. Thou preparest a table before me in the presence of mine enemies: thou anointest my head with oil; my cup runneth over. Surely goodness and mercy shall follow me all the days of my life: and I will dwell in the house of the Lord forever.*

Pillar 2

*I*t takes time to process thoughts and emotions, but we don't always take the time we need to reflect and heal. Learning to recognize —and listen to—that small voice can be the difference between life and death, surviving and thriving.

MY STORY

After my daughter came into this world in October 2000, I was not ready. Pregnancy was amazing, but motherhood was something else entirely. I instantly wanted my life back. I was not prepared for all that being a mother entailed: sleepless nights; crying; and finding a balance between work, life, and relationship that now included a baby. I was suffering from postpartum depression while trying to raise a child. The excitement that I thought I would feel had become a burden of the responsibilities. My boyfriend was always working, so he was not home as much as I would have liked for him to be and it felt like everything fell on me.

My days would start at five o'clock in the morning. I would get my daughter prepared for daycare and take a cab to drop her off at six. From there, I took a bus to get to the train station, and a train to get to work where I stayed from 8:30 a.m. to 4:30 p.m. The schedule actually worked in my favor because I was able to pick her up by 6 p.m. I did all of this while I was big as a house. My mind was always thinking about what I was going to cook for dinner that evening and how I was going to get my daughter to sleep in her own bed so I could sleep in mine. All so I could do it all over again the next day. And the day after that. I had to make sure her needs were met while still fighting the postpartum depression that I didn't know how to get rid of.

I found out I was pregnant with my second child in April 2001. I was still trying to get my life together with my daughter, but I wanted my child. Even though my life wasn't where I thought it was going to be, this new baby was coming. I was a ball of emotions. I remember feeling angry, upset, tired, and stressed all at the same time. Some days, I just wondered how I was going to do this. I wanted my boyfriend to be there for us more but he was running his own business that took up a lot of his time. I didn't want his work to suffer. I let him know that he could hold down the business, but I would need some more help.

My pregnancies weren't easy. They weren't just emotionally taxing on me, but also physically. I had early labor pains the month prior to delivery. I was one of those people who didn't speak what I was going through. I was trying not to be stressed, but anything outside of my planned routines would throw me off. If my daughter didn't sleep, I would be stressed. Having contractions when I was supposed to be planning my firstborn's party stressed me. I was on an emotional rollercoaster. I didn't have a choice to get off of it so I just had to plow through. So many people were relying on me.

The day after September 11, I was still in shock. I was just watching the news over and over again as they replayed the previous day's events. I questioned why I kept watching the images. I was there. I'd seen it all happen firsthand. I started my day on September 12 like nothing was different. As I was getting ready to go to work, I acted as if nothing would be different. I got up early and did my same morning routine because no one had called me to tell me otherwise. In my mind, there was no reason to assume that I shouldn't go to work. It didn't occur to me that the building I worked in was in the middle of Ground Zero.

I can't describe the smell of New York City when I stepped out of my home and made my way to work that day. I'd never smelled death before, but I knew that was it the moment I inhaled. The stench of burning metal, flesh, and fuel hung in the air during my entire trip. The most eerie feeling loomed. It was like something out of the Twilight Zone or a Hollywood movie. The atmosphere was surreal and clouded with sadness compared to how beautiful the previous day had started before the attack. It was dark and raining like the whole world was literally crying. It was like being in a nightmare I couldn't wake up from because it was not a dream.

A sadness came over me during my commute. I thought, if I just shake my head really quick and I open my eyes, this will all be a dream. So I did. It wasn't. It was quite overwhelming.

Once I got off the train, I saw all the men and women with the National Guard. I took notice of them but kept moving and went on my way to work. There was a lot of rubble around and a lot of fires that you were still burning. There was just so much ash. It was impossible to inhale without taking it into my lungs, but I tried to avert my eyes so I didn't have to see it everywhere, too.

I made my way upstairs to the office. It was empty except for a few of the uniformed members of the service. My desk was just as I'd left it. Even the bagel and tea I'd grabbed for breakfast was still there, undisturbed. I sat down and tried to comprehend what just happened. The office was eerily quiet. There were no people walking along the streets and the typical chatter I was used to was absent.

One of the lieutenants pointed out to me that we didn't know what could be in the air and, therefore, what we were breathing in. By then, I was six months pregnant and I was grateful that he was trying to protect me and my unborn child. I wasn't there much longer after that. He had a female detective escort me home.

As we were driving, there was nobody—and I mean nobody—on the bridge. The only cars on the road were silent police cars with their lights on. Being on the bridge this time was different from the day before. New York is known to always be this super busy place with millions of people around. I had never been on any of the city's bridges, no matter what time of day it was, and not seen a single soul. No one on a bridge. I believe that's when it finally struck me that the world was forever changed. September 11 was not only going to affect my life, but everyone else's life going forward.

Many people questioned why I even went to work the next day. Despite all of the confusion and anger and fear in the city and across the country, I felt it was my duty. Even though I didn't wear a uniform and I didn't carry a gun, I was a civilian member of the Police Commissioner's Office, a MOS (Member of the Service). I worked for the top person in the department who supervised and supported more than 40,000 cops. It was our duty to find out certain things. We needed to know what happened, why it happened, what we missed, and what we were going to do going forward. We had to figure out how to heal a city. I could have contacted my boss and said I was going to stay home the day after the tragic event, but I was there to do my job.

Yes, I was pregnant, but pregnancy had nothing to do with duty to me. As much knocking as the police get from the public and from government officials, when it comes down to traumatic events, I think that's where we show up the most.

We let New York City know we didn't run. We ran toward the disaster, not from it. For instance, when the World Trade Center was hit from the bottom in 1993, I was at work. I didn't go home that day either. I stayed because that was my job, my duty. I was more than willing to do what was needed. When you join an entity like the police force, you take an oath to do what's needed and you take that oath seriously, even if it means doing so at your own expense. So it never crossed my mind that I was potentially exposing myself, my boyfriend, and our children to harmful substances from the terror attack.

Nonetheless, this situation was different. I wasn't pregnant in 1993. When we were told that the area wasn't safe for non-uniformed MOS, I didn't fight it. I wanted my child and me to be safe. I tried to stay in touch with the office as much as I could from home. It didn't dawn on me that the day before I might have been exposed to certain elements or toxins or that I had potentially endangered my children and husband because of my exposure.

I was watching the news a lot while I was at home. I did my best to keep in touch with colleagues from my office, especially the civilian staff. I wanted to make sure that we were kept in the loop regarding when it would be safe for us to go back to the office.

During that time of waiting, I prioritized my daughter over everything and hugged her as much as possible. It wasn't lost on me that the decision to listen to my intuition could have saved my life. Had I stopped in that donut shop, I may not have been alive to sit at home on my couch and hug my daughter. I wouldn't have had the luxury of seeing her face or continuing to nurture the son I was still growing inside of my belly. The decision to change what I would get for breakfast stayed with me. That one choice changed my life. When you want to go against the grain or when the little voice is telling you not to do something, nine times out of ten it's for your own good. Don't do it. Not responding to it quickly enough can cause an outcome that you could never imagine. When you don't listen to that little voice, you will usually regret it. I am so happy that I made the decision to listen.

I like to call that voice the Lord or the Spirit. Others may call it something else, but the Spirit will never lead you astray. I went to work as opposed to going to the World Trade Center for breakfast that day. I was very grateful for taking the time to listen to my intuition and let the Spirit lead me away from danger. Nothing was lost on me.

When I think about it today, the day after September 11 could have been a whole different scenario had I not listened to the Spirit's quiet voice telling me to go straight into the office. After what felt like a lifetime, I took time and I cried. I sat with the tears, the pain, and the joy. The joy that my family and I were still here. The joy that I was still carrying life and my daughter was still able to run around and play. Although I had a lot of emotions, I didn't cry a lot. Not as much as you'd expect from a pregnant woman who had just witnessed the most deadly terror attack on American soil in history. But I did cry.

My life and my son's life could have been taken prematurely because I made one decision based on a temptation.

I was already running late for work that day. Had I been on time, I may have felt more comfortable standing in line to wait for the breakfast I really thought I wanted. Had that happened, I may have never made it out of the building. There are so many what-ifs, so many "shoulda, woulda, coulda" thoughts that cross my mind. All I know is that I made the right choice that day and listening to the Spirit led me to life.

MY LESSON

I refused to sit at home feeling helpless. I found my purpose while I was on that couch making calls and connecting people as best I could. It was my job to uplift, inspire, and support others who may have been going through trauma. It was my duty to be to others what I needed. I wanted to let them know that they were still here for a reason. Ultimately, I realized there was something bigger than myself that I had to engage in and find out about.

THE BLESSING

I kept my sanity in a time when the entire country was filled with fear. I was gifted with the ability to comfort others and remind them that hope still existed and our city was the most resilient in the world. Everything wasn't easy for me in the aftermath of 9/11, but the Lord strengthened me just enough to offer strength to others. The blessing was in the lesson for me.

THE AFFIRMATION

I was born with purpose and live to align myself with that purpose. I've been called to serve because I am worthy.

REFLECTION QUESTIONS

1. How would you react the day after a catastrophic event?

    _____

    _____

    _____

2. Do you need someone by your side to feel better?

    _____

    _____

    _____

3. Should you talk about it?

    _____

    _____

    _____

4. Is not talking about it a sign something is wrong?

    _____

    _____

    _____

5. When is it appropriate to talk about things?

_____

_____

_____

6. Even if you feel something is not wrong, should you seek out help?

_____

_____

_____

7. Would you want your significant other to approach you about the event or wait for you to come to them?

_____

_____

_____

8. Is work even on your mind after a catastrophic event?

_____

_____

_____

9.   Do you feel a duty to go back to work?

_____

_____

_____

10. Do you expect other people to come to your aid if they find out you were a part of the event?

_____

_____

_____

11. Should your job offer some counseling?

_____

_____

_____

Psalm 27:1-4 *The Lord is my light and my salvation; whom shall I fear? the Lord is the strength of my life; of whom shall I be afraid? When the wicked, even mine enemies and my foes, came upon me to eat up my flesh, they stumbled and fell. Though a host should encamp against me, my heart shall not fear: though war should rise against me, in this will I be confident. One thing have I desired of the Lord, that will I seek after; that I may dwell in the house of the Lord all the days of my life, to behold the beauty of the Lord, and to enquire in his temple.*

Pillar 3

*P*eace means everything on a healing journey. For some of us, it's the catalyst. For others, it's the destination. And for others, there are pit stops of peace along the way that make the journey bearable. I found my peace in God's Word. Where is yours?

MY STORY

As the days went on, I would wake up in the mornings and think— just for a flash—that the events of that day were just a terrible dream. As soon as I turned on the TV each day, I got confirmation that it was all real. But even though I'd see the reality in front of me, it was still so hard for me to accept. Hollywood hadn't even made something so unimaginable yet.

Once I began to digest it all, I was able to emotionally connect to the events of the day more. I learned that one of my best friends had close family in one of the towers. We prayed together that they made it out, but things were still so chaotic that it was hard to account for loved ones. They could have been injured in a hospital somewhere and there was no way to identify them yet. For days, I was on pins and needles, waiting to find out if they made it out of the building before it collapsed.

For the next 11 days, heroes pushed aside their own feelings of grief and fear while they dug through the rubble. They found so many bodies but every now and then, they'd find a survivor who managed to stay alive in a pocket of air or through some other miracle. Those miracles slowed down and then they stopped. It was hard to accept that they weren't going to find any more survivors in the wreckage. My best friend's godbrother and girlfriend were among those in the towers. When the family could not get in touch with them on that day, we had to contemplate the worst while trying to hold on to our faith.

At some point, I realized that I was only re-traumatizing myself by watching the footage of the planes hit the towers over and over again. And then watching them fall over and over again. I was there. I'd watched it from my office window. I'd been in the streets with my coworkers and fellow citizens while we walked aimlessly, not knowing if any place in the city would be safe for us.

It took years for me to really see how much of a dark place I was in back in those first days after the attack. I was probably moving on autopilot, but I thought I was more numb than low at the time. In hindsight, COVID-19 has taught us so much about the importance of clean air. No one wore masks after 9/11 unless they were actually at Ground Zero. Who knew what toxins we were exposing ourselves to, allowing the terror on our city to be extended far beyond the events that happened on September 11? It didn't help that the EPA told us that our air was safe. Obviously, it wasn't safe. We just didn't know that at the time.

I spent more of my time thinking about the future. I knew that the world would not be the same, and I was trying to figure out where to go next. There was so much uncertainty. I never wanted to be in a position where my children weren't safe. Maybe that meant that I should leave law enforcement, but I had job security and a sense of duty. I had so many decisions to make for my household while I was still trying to deal with the demons of watching the tragedy replay on every screen I saw, day in and day out.

It seemed as if every time I wrapped my head around one aspect of what I'd witnessed, some detail would come to light that would shake me. I just didn't know how to grasp it.

By the time we learned that the announcement about the air quality being safe wasn't right and that we'd all been breathing in dangerous particles, I was a few months away from delivering my son. The scientists said that pregnant women who were exposed to Ground Zero may have babies with mental or physical ailments. I wasn't sure how or if I was going to handle it. My life as a working wife and mother to one child was tough enough. I couldn't imagine adding a second child who had special needs. And it would be all my fault because I was breathing in all the things in the air while I was trying to make it home that day.

I had to deal with the guilt of potentially exposing my baby to harmful conditions and the guilt over worrying about how much my life would change if my baby had special mental or physical needs when I knew I was already exhausted. I still didn't even know I was having a little boy yet, and I was already obsessing over the ways I'd failed my child. I prayed to God that the baby wouldn't be affected.

I'd returned to work in the office when I got a call from my doctor. My medical team was monitoring my pregnancy more closely after the news about New York's air quality came out. I'd recently had a routine blood test and was anxiously awaiting the results when I got the call that said there was a chance that the baby may have Down syndrome. I just collapsed uncontrollably into tears while I was on the phone. I couldn't stop. I thanked the doctor for letting me know, and I hung up the phone.

As soon as I did, I heard a whisper in my ear. The voice said, "There's nothing wrong with the baby. The baby's fine."

In an instant, I was okay because once again, the Spirit was guiding me and comforting me. That changed everything. I was still upset, but I stopped crying. I knew that the doctor said one thing, but the Lord told me something else. I was going to go with what the Lord said because the Lord had not steered me wrong yet. I had just received confirmation that they were wrong. The doctors were wrong.

When my son was born on the 28th of December, he was a healthy baby. I was happy because the Lord was always watching out for us. The Spirit was the same Spirit that said "Go to work, don't go to the World Trade Center to get Krispy Kreme."

I was quite happy and quite content. When my son was born, I learned something more about the Lord: He truly does have the last say. I learned to lean on Him a lot more than I had ever done before.

MY LESSON

I have learned to trust the Spirit more and more day by day as I see the amazing things in my life. I listen to that still small voice. It was just the softest whisper in my ear that calmed me down on the phone that day. You should never have so much noise in your life that you can't hear when the Lord is speaking to you.

THE BLESSING

When you're pregnant or when you have children, it is not about what you want. It's about what's best for them. Sometimes you have to put yourself aside to put them first because they didn't ask to be born. We choose to bring them here, and we don't always know when we're making mistakes or potentially causing them harm. Every day they live to smile, in spite of their parents' shortcomings, is a blessing.

THE AFFIRMATION

I am an imperfect person with a desire to give a perfect love. I am capable of making mistakes that don't compromise my capacity to love.

REFLECTION QUESTIONS

1. Do you think it is best to try to understand the event? Why?

_____

_____

_____

2. If not directly involved in the event would you be concerned with the health of your child?

_____

_____

_____

3. Would you blame yourself if any issues came about with your child?

_____

_____

_____

4. Would the idea that something is wrong with you internally ever come across your mind?

_____

_____

_____

5. How soon should you go to the doctor?

_____

_____

_____

6. Could you ever feel normal if there was an issue with your child?

_____

_____

_____

7. Would you try to distance yourself from the event?

_____

_____

_____

8. Would there be a fear this event would happen again?

_____

_____

_____

9. Who do you blame for 9/11?

10. Is it your job to deal with your issues or is it your close friends and family?

11. Is life easy to go back to after an event like 9/11? Why or why not?

Philippians 4:7 *And the peace of God, which passeth all understanding, shall keep your hearts and minds through Christ Jesus.*

Pillar 4

The human tendency to turn on fight or flight mode in stressful situations is so real. Self-preservation sometimes requires running like I had to on 9/11. But what does self-preservation look like when it requires you to stand your ground?

MY STORY

Moving away from New York City was never my intention.

When the attack happened in New York, it made some people immediately re-evaluate their living arrangements. They didn't want to stay where something like this could happen and they wanted to move to a different place. That was understandable, but that wasn't me. I've been here all my life. I didn't want to leave and have to go and start all over again in a new place. At that point, I had 11 to 12 years on the force, and I wanted to finish my career with the department. Why make a major change when I was doing so well in my career? I had great benefits, I liked my work, I liked who I worked for, and I liked my coworkers. I was on high alert, but I didn't want to leave my home.

I saw the city differently after the attack. Everyone wasn't selfishly going on about their day without speaking to one another. Life slowed down for a bit, and I could see that everybody actually cared about one another. Everybody was kinder to each other. Everybody looked out for each other regardless of race because we were all upset. We were all angry. We all lost people. That tragic event brought people together from all walks of life. We all had a common denominator: We were survivors. And we wanted to find out who did this heinous act so we could see them brought to justice.

People actually wanted to care about the next person. We made a conscious decision to show up for one another. There was no ill intent behind caring for someone else, and I say that as a New Yorker because they say New Yorkers are tough and rough. No matter how you may perceive a New Yorker to be, this tragedy brought everyone together. It was terrible that something so horrible had to happen to make people across the city, country, and world pause to be more kind to each other.

The events of September 11 could have happened anywhere. That's why I had no interest in leaving. Other parts of our country were attacked that day. What good would it do for all of us to just move elsewhere? You can't keep moving because something bad happened. Will you move every time bad things show up in your life? You can't run forever. You have to stand, fight, pray, and be prepared for the next thing because there's always going to be something else. Devastating things can happen in any state or city around the world. When you think of the loss of life that the world had, also think of all the people that were on the planes that were hijacked. They weren't in a specific city, only planning to meet loved ones, go on a trip, go to work, and the list goes on and on.

My faith is my security and my security is in the Lord. Regardless of all the things that happened in New York, I am still here. My family is still here. All I can do is continue to rely on my faith, be vigilant, and just be more aware of my surroundings.

MY LESSON

Whatever comes around the corner is going to arrive because it was always there. Fortunately, we're able to control how we respond and that dictates the kind of person we want to be. Don't let fear or doubt paralyze you. Unfortunate circumstances and devastating events should not be the cause of you not walking into your purpose.

That attack and aftermath could have paralyzed me for the rest of my life. I could have chosen to live in fear. Instead, I choose not to let fear or doubt overtake me.

No matter what happens or what's thrown at you, it's up to you to decide if you are going to let it hit you. If it does hit you, do you just lay down and die, or do you get back up and keep going until you can't go anymore? Fear and doubt may arise in you, but you can't stay there. You can't live in the space of always being in fear. It's called life. It's gonna happen. You can't control everything. How you live that life will dictate your legacy.

MY BLESSING

I want you to know that whatever happens in your life, whether it is devastating or not, you're here to tell the story.

THE AFFIRMATION

In good times and in not-so-good times, I show up as my authentic, loving self. It doesn't take tragedy for me to give my best to the people around me.

REFLECTION QUESTIONS

1. If you were alive for 9/11, do you feel anything changed in your life?

_____

_____

_____

2. Did you experience a new fear in your life after 9/11?

_____

_____

_____

3. How on guard were you after the attack?

_____

_____

_____

4. Did you lose someone during the 9/11 attack?

_____

_____

_____

5. Would a catastrophic event make you feel like something in your life needs to change?

_____

_____

_____

6. Would there be a deeper appreciation of life?

_____

_____

_____

7. What significant changes would you make to your life?

_____

_____

_____

8. Do you feel anything has changed in the country?

_____

_____

_____

9. Do you feel more or less safe?

_____

_____

_____

10. Does flying hold any trauma?

_____

_____

_____

11. Do you fear another 9/11 will happen?

_____

_____

_____

Revelation 22:13 *I am Alpha and Omega, the beginning and the end, the first and the last.*

Pillar 5

W hen you're feeling lost, they say the best place to find answers is to open a book. Opening this one was a great start.

MY STORY

I looked to the Bible for answers to why this was happening, even if it was just a scripture a day. On the days I didn't actually go into the Bible, I would recite Psalm 23 to myself. That one chapter helped me to get past the events of September 11 and beyond. When I couldn't sleep, I'd pray as I lay in bed. It's a prayer I've known since childhood and it's become my foundation.

Scripture gave me strategies I could use to get through my everyday life. Nothing in scripture or the world can make someone just "get over" the kind of trauma I experienced, but it definitely helped me learn to adapt to my new normal.

Women in the Bible helped me to see myself clearly. Men in those stories went through their fair share of hardships and challenges, but it was the women who had to face things that were meant to destroy them. They refused to allow it to happen. Even through their subservience to men, these Biblical women showed their strength when they were faced with adversity. They could have given up but they didn't because they wanted to honor God and be the support their children and families needed. I wanted to be that kind of woman too, so I found solace in the Bible.

There were Psalms I could draw on for my own strength. If I was feeling down, unworthy, or scared, the 91st or the 92nd chapters were there for me. I relied on Psalms 27 and 23 as much. The Bible taught me that whatever you go through, you're not going through it alone. The Spirit is always with you. You just have to invite Him in to show you and help you get through whatever circumstances are troubling or affecting you or clouding your mind. The Bible taught me that no matter what, there is a light at the end of the tunnel. You may not see it that day, you may not see it the next day, but you will eventually be basking in light. When you look back, you'll be amazed at how you got through it, but not why.

When the Spirit is guiding and protecting you, it's easy to marvel at the grace extended over your life. There's rarely a moment I look up and don't immediately know that God is the source of that grace over my life. Connecting with the Spirit through the Bible helps me to get through the tough and depressing times. It helps me to get through adversity. I was aware of the Bible before September 11, but I wasn't connected to it the way I am now.

My personal Bible study taught me that my understanding of parables and scripture may have been new, but my connection with the Spirit had always been with me. It had saved my life on September 11 and it had allowed me to keep going when things seemed impossible. My connection had ripple effects on my marriage, our children, my job, and my community. I found even more strength than I already had because I confirmed that I was never alone.

MY LESSON

The person who looks back at you in the mirror is counting on you as well as your children because they look to you as inspiration. If we show strength, then they'll endure. I witnessed what should have killed my mom but it didn't. So no matter what I go through in life, I can look at her and all she's been through, and she is still here. There's nothing that is ever going to happen to me that will prevent me from living my best life and leaving a lesson as well as a legacy for my children.

I guess a motivational speaker would be the best role for me. I would just have to get over that fear of speaking in public, but it's a story that needs to be heard because so many people keep their feelings to themselves, myself included. If I'm able to bring it out of you, even if it's just one person, that's a win for me. That's one less person who will think about suicide. That's one less person going to drugs. That's one less person living life in a liquor bottle. That's one less person who will go through life thinking that they're not worthy of anything or anyone. That would be my purpose and my legacy going forward.

MY BLESSING

My newfound belief in Jesus allowed me to venture into fields I would not have previously been in. I always knew I was called to serve others, but my connection to the Spirit revealed a deeper purpose. I'm not a life coach, but I do feel called to inspire people. As I complete this book, I'm preparing myself for motivational speaking and other opportunities that I'm being led toward because if I'm still standing, I know everyone who reads this can overcome their obstacles as well.

THE AFFIRMATION

It doesn't matter if I have the books, the education, or the access anyone thinks I need. I'm connected to the Spirit, and that's enough to lead me where I'm meant to be.

REFLECTION QUESTIONS

1. Who do you hold responsible for 9/11?

   _____

   _____

   _____

2. Is religion a big part of your life?

   _____

   _____

   _____

3. How does religion help when experiencing trauma?

   _____

   _____

   _____

4. After catastrophic events, is it natural to turn toward religion?

   _____

   _____

   _____

5. Do you blame religion for the events of 9/11?

_____

_____

_____

6. What is one positive thing about religion?

_____

_____

_____

7. What is one negative thing about religion?

_____

_____

_____

8. Should the actions of one group of people cause outrage amongst a group of people who observe the same religion?

_____

_____

_____

9. Should religion play a role in everyday life?

_____

_____

_____

10. Does America come together for 9/11?

_____

_____

_____

11. How has 9/11 changed your approach to life?

_____

_____

_____

Proverbs 31:10 *Who can find a virtuous woman? For her price is far above rubies.*

Pillar 6

Our priorities shift over time just as much as the puzzle pieces that make up our lives do. There is beauty in the journey of learning about yourself and a reward when you finally start to give yourself what you need.

MY STORY

It was clear to anyone paying attention that I prioritized giving to others over taking care of myself, but that was not obvious to me. Somehow I must have started looking at my boyfriend as an extension of myself because we went through a difficult time. I was going through so much emotionally, but he was also going through things in his life that caused him to place me on the back burner. It made me resentful. I had so much on my plate already, and it's even harder when you have to do that alone. I realized that I needed to start making myself a priority or I wasn't going to make it.

It took me a lot of years to figure out that I had to start taking care of Vanessa if I was going to be any good to anyone else. The saying is true: You can't pour from an empty cup. But even when I was able to come to that realization, there were still demands on my life as a wife and mother that made it difficult to put myself first. My husband became ill starting with a stroke in 2018, open heart surgery in 2021, and a blood clot in the heart in 2022. I was trying to keep myself sane and out of dark places while being a caregiver to my husband. It was not easy and at times, I was on the verge of a nervous breakdown. I've learned to place greater value on the small moments I have to myself. Sometimes that's reading a book, praying and writing, or maybe just going out for a walk. I discovered that I desperately needed to make time for myself, and it was hard.

Kids are always watching you. People would laugh and think I was trying to tell a funny joke when I said my kids saw me when they woke up and when they went to sleep before they moved out of the house for college. Their father often came home while they were still in school, engaged in other activities, or late at night. I became the parent they relied on. If I was ever late getting home from work, my phone would blow up with calls and texts. They didn't call their father in the same way because they realized the dedication to his business and it was ok. My boyfriend did his best to be there to help raise and nurture them. It was an added strain when he was not there. I struggled to handle it all because I was going through so much already and that was an extremely tough time to endure. I got through it thanks to a lot of prayer and a lot of going to church. There was a lot of crying and a lot of writing, too.

I was going through so much emotionally, physically, and mentally. I was trying to recover from postpartum depression while carrying my second child and then lived through the September 11 terror attacks. Then I had to somehow raise two kids in the midst of PTSD and the depression that followed. I felt really lost, and I didn't know what to do.

It was those feelings of uncertainty and pain that led me to turn toward the Bible. I was just looking for answers and ended up finding that and more. I also found that writing was a healthy outlet for me around this time, and I wrote a lot. I listened to gospel music, and I prayed a lot. I did everything I could to release all that was pent up in me. That included crying lots of tears, too.

MY LESSON

Prioritizing myself allowed me to learn about myself in ways I didn't know before. I knew Vanessa the Girlfriend. I knew Vanessa the Mom. Parts of me remembered Vanessa the Girl, but Vanessa the Woman was completely foreign to me. When I finally took time for myself with the same kind of intention that I cared for everyone else in my life, I learned what I needed. I learned how to feed my body, my spirit, and my heart. From that lesson came the beginning of my healing.

THE BLESSING

Taking time for myself led me to writing. Once again, the still small voice of the Spirit told me I needed to have more alone time. That led me to more time in the Bible and eventually to writing. God blessed me with an outlet and an opportunity all at once.

THE AFFIRMATION

Answering the call to serve means caring for myself first. I am committed to loving myself with the same fierceness that I love the people around me.

REFLECTION QUESTIONS

1. What are the benefits of having a reliable partner?

    _____

    _____

    _____

2. Should a partner try to help or simply listen to the struggles of their partners?

    _____

    _____

    _____

3. Should a significant other take time away from work to be there for their partner when experiencing trauma?

    _____

    _____

    _____

4. Can a partner make a situation worse?

    _____

    _____

    _____

5.   How should a partner approach helping?

_____

_____

_____

6.   Does a traumatic event make a relationship stronger or weaker?

_____

_____

_____

7.   Is love the necessary ingredient to help overcome trauma?

_____

_____

_____

8.   What are ways to begin the healing process?

_____

_____

_____

9. Is it understandable if the partner feels overwhelmed by their traumatized partner's altered mindset?

_____

_____

_____

10. Do the untraumatized partner's feelings come into play at any point?

_____

_____

_____

11. Are there other people you can seek out for help?

_____

_____

_____

Joshua 1:9 *Have not I commanded thee? Be strong and of a good courage; be not afraid, neither be thou dismayed: for the Lord thy God is with thee withersoever thou goest.*

Pillar 7

The moment you start to uncover the truth behind who you are, you start to see deeper truths in the things that shaped you along the way. If you're going to reflect on the past, it's important to look through your healed lens of the present and not through the vision of your past.

MY STORY

The more I healed the trauma of my adulthood, the more I started to see that much of my childhood was full of different kinds of trauma. I just never considered what I experienced to be anything other than normal.

When I was growing up, my father was rarely home. When he was, he was either very combative with my sister and brothers and/or combative with our mom. He drank and smoked a lot, so our home was filled with significant confusion and dysfunction. On top of that, I was bullied in school. I didn't feel there was a safe place for me to go physically or emotionally. People's opinions of me and their harmful words became my perspective of the person looking back at me in the mirror.

My feelings of loneliness continued into adulthood, and my unhealthy responses didn't go away. They only grew up with me. I was hooking up with people who were emotionally abusive, but I never told anyone about it. I pretty much built a wall around myself. I was an ice princess with a fortress that no one could penetrate unless I chose to let them come in. Some bad examples of humanity had taught me that I couldn't trust anybody because they would only hurt me. I just built that wall around myself instead.

Now I've developed introverted and extroverted parts of my personality. There are times when I want to be social and other times when I want to be private. Nurturing both sides has made all the difference for me.

MY LESSON

I learned how to take charge when I was very young. Being the firstborn of four children to a single mother will do that. I was expected to take charge and to know what to do, so I did. But that sense of responsibility and the anxiety that came with it followed me like a shadow until I woke up to my healing.

THE BLESSING

The healing journey is not easy, but it is worth it. As you heal, you will start to see the world in a new light. You will be able to identify the things that have been holding you back and start to let them go. You will also be able to see the beauty in the world and appreciate the things that you have.

The blessing of healing is that it allows you to live a more fulfilling life. You will be able to connect with others on a deeper level and build stronger relationships. You will also be able to find your purpose in life and make a difference in the world.

If you are struggling with trauma, don't give up. Healing is possible. Take one step at a time and be patient with yourself. With time and effort, you will be able to overcome your trauma and live a happy, fulfilling life.

THE AFFIRMATION

I am aware of my past and free to create the life and future I want to see for myself.

REFLECTION QUESTIONS

1. Should familymembers be available to help at all times?

_____

_____

_____

2. How can family members make things worse?

_____

_____

_____

3. Who are you closest to in your family?

_____

_____

_____

4. Do you feel they are always there for you?

_____

_____

_____

5. Is it appropriate to always come to them with your problems?

_____

_____

_____

6. Can they come to you with their problems?

_____

_____

_____

7. Is it the job of the family to help you through your trauma?

_____

_____

_____

8. If not family, do you have a reliable safe zone? Who?

_____

_____

_____

9. What is your opinion about talking about your feelings?

_____

_____

_____

10. Does therapy work?

_____

_____

_____

11. Is it other people's job to help you, or do you need to help yourself?

_____

_____

_____

Ephesians 3:20-21 *Now unto Him that is able to do exceeding abundantly above all that we ask or think according to the power that worketh in us. Unto Him be glory in the church by Christ Jesus throughout all ages, world without end. Amen.*

Pillar 8

Our communities make a difference in how we live our lives. Whether it's your neighborhood, your faith community, or coworkers, the people around you are a reflection of the life you want to live. When things aren't going well, they're the people who can make the difference between scratching to survive and freeing yourself to thrive.

MY STORY

After 9/11, I felt a strong need to connect with others who had been through similar experiences. I started doing inspirational and motivational videos on social media to help survivors of any trauma. I also started attending therapy to deal with my feelings with regard to the attacks.

Through therapy, I realized how many amazing people also are struggling to cope with the aftermath of that day. I share my story, pain, and hopes for the future. The decision to help others began to have a healing effect on me as well. It gave me a deeper sense of purpose and belonging to fulfill my assignment that the Lord placed within me.

When we help others, we help ourselves. By giving our time and energy to others, we can find healing and hope in the midst of our own struggles. I might not ever be able to completely forgive the people who contributed to 9/11, but I've learned to forgive their misguided ideology. I know there's no way that the God who protected me that day is the same who told them to fly airplanes into the World Trade Center. As I came to that conclusion, I realized that I hadn't forgiven myself.

I had unconsciously carried so much guilt over the way I handled myself that day and in the months that followed. I felt guilty over being tempted to stop for a donut that moment, even though I listened to the Spirit when I was told to go straight to the office. I felt guilty for not thinking to cover my mouth and nose as I walked through the streets and across the bridge. I felt guilty for dedicating so much of my time to connecting with colleagues and coworkers when my daughter needed me and my boyfriend had experienced his own issues. I felt guilty for potentially harming my unborn child and, when he was born, I felt guilty for being depressed.

Then, there was the survivor's guilt.

I thought about all those people who lost their lives on that day. I questioned why I survived by not going to the World Trade Center as planned. I knew there had to be a reason, but not being able to see or understand it made me feel even more guilty for still being here. I bet someone died that day who already knew exactly what they were meant to do with their life had it not been cut so short. There had to be an assignment for my life but I was so sad. I didn't know what it was, or if I even wanted the assignment. I never believed I had the tools even to complete this assignment effectively.

I'd felt so sad and depressed for so long that it was routine. It was both eye-opening and earth-shattering to learn that I had been more impatient and unkind to myself than I had been to any other human I'd ever met. Recognizing and understanding that was one thing. Forgiving myself was another entirely.

It wasn't until I was on the brink of darkness and didn't want to live anymore that I realized I needed to accept reality: I had experienced a series of traumas throughout my life, but I had survived them all as best I could. I was able to begin moving on once I accepted the facts as they were.

Before 9/11, you couldn't keep me off a plane. I'm more jittery when I travel now, especially when I fly. Now I get a little skittish whenever a plane has turbulence, and I never used to.

But I also became more resilient after that day. My life's purpose came to me because of what I had been through, knowing that it could have gone another way. I had an epiphany. It was the Lord telling me there was an assignment for me and that it was time to engage in that assignment and purpose. I wasn't sure exactly what it was then, but I knew that I was saved to be here on this Earth for a reason. I did not make it out of there and live to now go back to my life as normal. Nothing could or would ever be the same for me. As time went on, I realized it and my purpose became clear to me.

Beyond that, I realized that I had to forgive all of the people who hurt me. Unfortunately, the list was long before I encountered terrorists on September 11. I made a conscious decision to release myself from my anger and resentment. I choose to live in peace and freedom instead.

Forgiveness is a powerful tool for healing. It allows us to let go of the anger and resentment that we may be holding onto. Eventually, I realized that harboring anger was only hurting me. It was preventing me from moving on with my life, so I made the decision to forgive them.

Forgiveness doesn't mean that I condone what they did. It simply means that I'm no longer going to let their actions control my life. Thankfully, I had a community of people around me, especially my husband and children, to remind me that I was worthy.

MY LESSON

I was a stressed-out, one-woman team, so it's no wonder that I went through depression. You can't choose the life you are given or how God will use you, but you can choose to trust the process. You may not know or understand your purpose just yet, but keep the faith and seek answers to your questions. One day, you will understand and you will be the light in someone else's darkness.

THE BLESSING

The blessing of community is that it provides us with a support system of people who understand what we're going through. We can lean on each other for strength and encouragement. We can also find comfort in knowing that we're not alone. In times when it's difficult to forgive others or ourselves, our communities can lend us their courage.

THE AFFIRMATION

I am a part of a community of survivors. We are strong, resilient, and hopeful. Together, we can heal and build a better future.

REFLECTION QUESTIONS

1. Can someone ever truly move on from 9/11?

_____

_____

_____

2. How can untreated trauma affect someone's life?

_____

_____

_____

3. Is trauma treatable?

_____

_____

_____

4. Can someone truly understand 9/11 if they were not there?

_____

_____

_____

5. Is hatred always the dominant emotion when something bad happens?

    _____

    _____

    _____

6. How can people learn to come together instead of dividing themselves?

    _____

    _____

    _____

7. Should the government help those who now suffer from health problems because of 9/11?

    _____

    _____

    _____

8. How do you personally deal with trauma?

    _____

    _____

    _____

9. Do you think other people should adopt your method?

_____

_____

_____

10. Has the country truly moved on from 9/11?

_____

_____

_____

11. Do you believe peace in the world is truly possible?

_____

_____

_____

Isaiah 54:17-18 *No weapon formed against thee will prosper; and every tongue that shall rise against thee in judgment thou shalt condemn. This is the heritage of the servants of the Lord, and their righteousness is of me, saith the Lord.*

Pillar 9

MY STORY

Years after 9/11, New York and the world were hit with another trau-matic tragedy. When the pandemic hit, it was hard.

As someone who is called to serve others, I was more concerned about the health of my family, my friends, and my coworkers than myself. I did everything in my power to make sure my boyfriend stayed safe. Our children were away in school, so I insisted they get vaccinated as soon as they were eligible. The first responders in our department were also among the first to be eligible to take the vac-cine. I didn't think of myself as I worked to make sure the people around me were monitoring their health.

I didn't get vaccinated until it was announced that 9/11 survivors were particularly vulnerable to COVID-19. Health officials basically told us that we would die if we were exposed to the virus and unvac-cinated. They said vaccinated survivors shouldn't even end up in the hospital if they did contract the virus. When I did get sick, I was one of the vaccinated people who was able to ride out the illness at home and away from the dangers of hospitals.

When I got better and returned to work, there was a mask mandate for anyone who worked from the office. We had to put partitions around everybody's desks to make sure we weren't breathing in the same air. We made certain if somebody was sick, we were as protected as the science said we could be through the plexiglass. Work schedules were staggered for people who wanted to come later than their normal to avoid larger office crowds, which is what I did. I changed my tour from a 9 a.m. to 5 p.m. schedule to a 5 a.m. to 1 p.m. schedule because there was hardly anyone in the building.

There was an option to work from home but as I stepped back to reflect on all that was happening around me, it seemed like it may have just been time to retire. Between depression and PTSD, I was having more and more issues. Going to work had become such a burden for me because I couldn't sit for long periods of time as a result of the issues I had from 9/11. I was in a lot of pain. I was taking Uber to work because I couldn't take the subway, and I couldn't go up the stairs anymore. Part of me wanted to leave on my 55th birthday so I could access my pension but my quality of life had changed so much, I questioned what early retirement could look like for me. If I could have retired earlier, I would have, but I just didn't have that option. Now I just live every day as if it's going to be my last.

MY LESSON

I decided that whatever time I have left, I want to spend it with my children and husband, who I love dearly. A lot of people who got sick on the job during the pandemic are not here anymore. Others who got sick had a hard time recovering and are just trying to live day by day. Others are trying to live with 9/11-related illnesses that are still killing people today.

One of the detectives I worked with, the man who directed me to relay important information across the department before we evacuated our building on 9/11, died two years ago. He had cancer and was only in his 50s. So many coworkers, uniform and civilian, are still dealing with the tragedy of that day. Others have succumbed to illnesses they contracted.

Cherishing life means being grateful for our own and the lives of others. I grieve for all we've lost since September 11, but I'm also so grateful for all we've been blessed to experience in the years since.

MY BLESSING

While most of America was completely shocked and unprepared for the COVID-19 pandemic, New Yorkers like me had already seen that level of horror before. We knew what it was like to see our usually busy streets completely empty. We knew what it was like to come together for the common good. For all the ways the pandemic hurt us, we were prepared and knew we would survive because we'd survived once before.

THE AFFIRMATION

It's not about "making it." It's about gratitude for the opportunity to try. Thank you, Lord, for a chance to try.

REFLECTION QUESTIONS

1.   Do you feel the country's citizens are closer as a result of 9/11?

_____

_____

_____

2.   How important is family to you?

_____

_____

_____

3.   Can family help heal wounds?

_____

_____

_____

4.   If you have children, do they know about 9/11?

_____

_____

_____

5.   Is it important for children to know about 9/11?

_____

_____

_____

6.   Is 9/11 something you seek to remember or something to forget?

_____

_____

_____

7.   Is time the best thing to help heal wounds?

_____

_____

_____

8.   Did the pandemic traumatize you?

_____

_____

_____

9. Did the same fear from 9/11 re-emerge when the pandemic began?

_____

_____

_____

10. Do you have any lingering health issues from the pandemic?

_____

_____

_____

11. What tips would you give to others feeling pain?

_____

_____

_____

Romans 12:2 *And be not conformed to this world; but be ye transformed by the renewing of your mind that ye may prove what is that good, and acceptable, and perfect, will of God.*

Pillar 10

*H*ope is essential for healing. It gives us the strength to keep going when things are tough or obstacles feel insurmountable. Maybe the difference between impossible and possible is simply belief.

MY STORY

After 9/11, I lost hope for the future I envisioned for myself and my family. I knew that the world would never be the same. I also worried that my children would grow up in a world filled with more fear and violence than I ever had to see.

But eventually, I realized that I couldn't give up hope. I had to believe that things would get better. I had to have faith in the future, so I started to focus on the positive things in my life. I was grateful for my family, my friends, and my community. I also started to reframe the way I looked at things. Every person I interacted with when I volunteered had a chance to change the world, and something I said or did could have sparked something in them. Based on that way of thinking, I had countless opportunities to make a difference. Just by existing, I was creating a little more hope in the world. But it was only possible with the Spirit guiding me.

Sometimes I would say, "Lord, it's all on you." That was the best way I knew how to surrender.

In the years since September 11, my relationship with God has gotten deeper and stronger. I pray a lot, a whole lot. I play gospel music to keep my energy high. I recite a scripture if I need comfort. That especially came in handy when I had to get on a plane after the attacks. I thanked the Lord every time we touched back down safely. I'd take off with hope and He would answer my prayer for safe travel each time. That built my faith because I kept seeing the Lord show up for me when I was in need, even if the need was small, like reassurance that my children were okay in school that day.

Sometimes I felt stronger than others. Other times, I felt weaker. Regardless of how I'm feeling at any given moment, I'm always comforted with hope from the Spirit. I've had too many encounters with grace and protection to lose hope now, or ever again.

It's so important to focus on the positive, especially when we feel like we're surrounded by the negative. Focusing on negativity kills hope and any chance it could have. When we focus on the positive, we're more likely to see the possibilities for a better future. It's equally important to surround ourselves with positive people. Their hopefulness and optimism can help us to stay hopeful and optimistic ourselves.

It's also important to take action to create a better future. When we do, we're not only making a difference in the world, but we're also giving ourselves a sense of purpose and hope.

Having hope shouldn't mean abandoning reality. It's easier on the brain and the body to break our deepest desires and goals down into bite-sized pieces. It's key to be realistic as we do this. Take things one day at a time and watch your own faith deepen and grow.

MY LESSON

Hope is a choice. It's not easy to maintain hope in the face of adversity, but it's essential for our healing. When we have hope, we have the strength to keep going. We also have the ability to create a better future for ourselves and others.

If you're struggling to cultivate hope in your life, there are many resources available to help you. You can talk to a therapist, counselor, or spiritual advisor. You can also find many helpful books and articles on the topic of hope.

Remember, hope is essential for healing. When you have hope, you have the strength to keep going and create a better future for yourself and others.

THE BLESSING

The blessing of hope is that it gives us the strength to overcome challenges. It also allows us to see the beauty in the world and to believe in the possibility of a better future.

There are so many people dealing with trauma and difficulty. They may not have a person to lean on or to talk to. Maybe they have no way to express what is going on. Maybe they don't trust anyone enough to be vulnerable.

THE AFFIRMATION

I have hope for the future. I believe that things will get better. I am committed to creating a better world for myself and others.

REFLECTIVE QUESTIONS

1. Can hatred be the dominant emotion if someone wishes to heal?

_____

_____

_____

2. Is it possible to forgive those responsible for 9/11?

_____

_____

_____

3. Is forgiveness necessary?

_____

_____

_____

4. Can you heal any emotional wounds?

_____

_____

_____

5. What do you wish you had known on the day of 9/11?

    _____

    _____

    _____

6. Can you watch documentaries about 9/11?

    _____

    _____

    _____

7. Does the younger generation truly understand the events of 9/11?

    _____

    _____

    _____

8. How would you explain to the younger generation what experiencing or seeing 9/11 was truly like?

    _____

    _____

    _____

9.   Do 9/11 conspiracy theories frustrate you?

_____

_____

_____

10. Have you changed your thinking about 9/11?

_____

_____

_____

11. Did anyone ever reach out to you to offer their condolences?

_____

_____

_____

John 1:1 *In the beginning was the Word and the Word was with God, and the Word was God.*

Pillar 11

*T*he healing journey is lifelong, and it's not linear. There will be times when you feel like you're taking two steps forward and one step back. As long as you keep moving forward, you will reach your destination.

MY STORY

If you had told me on the night of September 11 that I would survive it and more, I might have asked for proof before I believed you. As I sat in my home and rocked my daughter against my pregnant belly, I found God in my gratitude. As I tried to process my emotions, I could only come back to an overwhelming feeling of thanks for being spared to hold her again.

Everything just happened so fast that day. It went from a normal Tuesday to the plane crash to the search and rescue efforts. It was all just so scary. The grief was unlike anything I'd ever felt before. I mourned for the friends, family, and coworkers I lost on 9/11. But I also struggled with understanding how people who were just at work, in the shops, or walking by had their lives ended. They didn't do anything wrong.

It took me a while to accept that it actually happened. It wasn't until I went to work the next day and was introduced to the smell of death that it really hit home. I began to admit to myself that it took place. All the cops were wearing rifles and bulletproof vests. New York looked like a police state, not my home. I got through it by moving on autopilot. Looking back, I think that was the first step in my healing: Self-preservation. But I couldn't stay in that state long.

Even when watching the news became too difficult for me and it seemed like I was going numb, I unintentionally punished myself. I kept watching it because every news channel had it on. It could have been a result of my survivor's guilt, but I couldn't seem to look away completely, especially once I acknowledged how much it hurt me to realize I was still alive to see the news. The people who I would have been in line with for donuts weren't alive. If I was grateful for my life, I thought that also meant being constantly mindful of all the lives lost.

Life cannot flourish in the midst of death. I had to break out of that, but I only had questions. Who did this to us? Why do they hate us so much? How did I survive? Why? Have I hurt my baby? Will my depression make me a bad mother? Why am I torturing myself this way?

I didn't have a single answer. That's when the Spirit led me to the Bible.

I saw myself and my pain reflected in some of those stories in scripture. In the places where I didn't see myself, I found inspiration. They went through so much, but everyone who had faith in God didn't just make it through, they had the most personal connections to God. I wanted that, so I started pursuing it.

Clearly, there were challenges along the way. Raising two kids under the age of two in the aftermath of the largest and most deadly terror attack on American soil was no joke. Doing that while feeling sad, lonely, overwhelmed, and depressed was a miracle. If I needed proof that God was real, I'd only have to look at my children. They have grown into amazing people, in spite of their circumstances. That truth brings me back to gratitude, too.

As the days after September 11 extended into weeks and then years, I learned more and more about the power of prayer and gratitude. I found strength in connecting with people, and I saw that everyone is created with a talent that they need to explore. I believe that exploration is what leads us to purpose.

It's not going to be easy, but it will always be rewarding. Like people say, if it was easy, everyone would do it. There are going to be obstacles thrown in your way. You can either let them stop you, or you can choose to step over that obstacle and keep going.

I want you to keep going.

Your legacy lies on the other side of your obstacle, on the other side of your pain. You have to be willing to ask questions first to find answers that will lead you to your legacy. You have a purpose. Other people can only get to theirs if you fulfill yours first.

MY LESSON

The hardest thing to learn in the time that has passed since September 11 has been patience. It seems like the most consistent lesson God has revealed to me over this time—from the patience and kindness we showed our neighbors in those first hours after the attacks to the patience I had to show myself as I moved through the stages of my grief.

I also had to learn that the same warm feeling I got from extending kindness to others was possible to feel if I only attempted to be kind to myself, too. Learning to take care of myself required me to build a real support system for myself.

THE BLESSING

The healing journey is filled with self-discovery and transformation. It's a journey of learning to love and accept yourself for who you are. It's a journey of finding your purpose in life and making a difference in the world.

THE AFFIRMATION

I am healed. I am joyous. I am whole.

REFLECTIVE QUESTIONS

1. If alive at the time of the attacks, what is one moment that sticks out to you from 9/11?

_____

_____

_____

2. What do you want to tell people about 9/11?

_____

_____

_____

3. Do you believe people take the events of 9/11 seriously in today's world?

_____

_____

_____

4. Is talking the only way to feel better or are there others? If so, what other options are there?

_____

_____

_____

5.   Is there a good place to go with the healing process?

_____

_____

_____

6.   Do you feel like there is still a chance another 9/11 could take place?

_____

_____

_____

7.   Do you tell people about your personal experience during 9/11?

_____

_____

_____

8.   What conspiracy theories have you heard about 9/11?

_____

_____

_____

9.   Does religion become more important later in life?

_____

_____

_____

10.   Do you feel like America is safe?

_____

_____

_____

11.   How much time would you need to feel that things had gotten back to normal?

_____

_____

_____

Conclusion

As I bring this journey to a close, I am reminded that the story of September 11, 2001, is not just one of loss and devastation but also of resilience, recovery, and rebirth. Over the past 23 years, I have learned that while the wounds from that day may never fully heal, they can be transformed into something powerful—a testament to the strength of the human spirit.

The path has been fraught with challenges, but through the darkness, I discovered the light of community, compassion, and the unwavering support of those who stood by my side. This journey has taught me that survivorship is not just about overcoming the past; it's about redefining the future with purpose, hope, and an unshakable belief in the possibility of renewal.

As I move forward, I carry with me the lessons learned and the memories of those who were lost, forever etched in my heart. This book was an attempt to make sense of a world forever changed, but it is also a tribute to the enduring spirit of those who lived through that day and to the countless acts of kindness and solidarity that have helped me—and so many others—rebuild our lives.

The journey continues, but now with a deeper understanding that even in the face of unimaginable adversity, there is always hope, and there is always a way to begin anew.there is always hope, and there is always a way to begin anew. No matter how daunting the challenges before us may seem, within each of us lies the strength to rise, rebuild, and rediscover the light that guides us forward. Every setback is an opportunity to cultivate resilience, and every moment of despair holds the seed of new beginnings. We are not defined by the obstacles we face but by how we choose to overcome them, embracing the possibilities that lie ahead with courage, faith, and an unwavering belief in our ability to create a brighter future. It is my hope that you will discover your power to triumph against all odds. Victory is yours for the taking.

11 Days of Triumph
Challenge

DAY 1

AFFIRM

I am capable of overcoming any challenge that comes my way.

REFLECT

What does resilience mean to you?

_____

_____

_____

_____

_____

_____

_____

How do you define success in terms of resilience?

_____

_____

_____

_____

_____

_____

What role does resilience play in achieving your goals?

_____

_____

_____

_____

_____

_____

_____

Can resilience be learned, or is it innate?

_____

_____

_____

_____

_____

_____

How do you bounce back from failure or setbacks?

_____

_____

_____

_____

_____

_____

What strategies do you use to maintain resilience during difficult times?

_____

_____

_____

_____

_____

_____

Have you ever faced a situation that tested your resilience? If so, how did you handle it?

_____

_____

_____

_____

_____

_____

DAY 2

AFFIRM

I trust in my ability to find solutions to any problem I encounter.

REFLECT

What are the key characteristics of resilient individuals?

_____

_____

_____

_____

_____

_____

How do you cultivate resilience in yourself and others?

_____

_____

_____

_____

_____

_____

What are the benefits of developing resilience?

_____

_____

_____

_____

_____

_____

How does resilience contribute to mental and emotional well-being?

_____

_____

_____

_____

_____

_____

Can resilience help in building stronger relationships?

_____

_____

_____

_____

_____

_____

What role does self-awareness play in developing resilience?

_____

_____

_____

_____

_____

_____

How do you stay motivated and optimistic during challenging
situations?

_____

_____

_____

_____

_____

_____

DAY 3

AFFIRM

I am resilient and can bounce back from setbacks stronger than ever.

REFLECT

What personal qualities or strengths have helped you overcome past challenges, and how can you leverage these in future setbacks?

_____

_____

_____

_____

_____

_____

Can you recall a specific setback you faced? What steps did you take to recover, and what did you learn from the experience?

_____

_____

_____

_____

_____

_____

How do you typically respond emotionally and mentally to setbacks? What strategies can you use to maintain a positive mindset during difficult times?

_____

_____

_____

_____

_____

_____

What role do your support systems—friends, family, mentors—play in your resilience? How can you strengthen these relationships to better support you in the future?

_____

_____

_____

_____

_____

In what ways have setbacks led to personal growth or new opportunities in your life? How can you shift your perspective to see challenges as opportunities for growth?

_____

_____

_____

_____

_____

What are some healthy coping mechanisms or self-care practices that help you stay resilient? How can you integrate these into your daily routine?

_____

_____

_____

_____

_____

How do you define success and failure? How can you reframe your understanding of setbacks to see them as a natural part of the journey toward your goals?

_____

_____

_____

_____

_____

DAY 4

AFFIRM

Every obstacle is an opportunity for growth and learning.

REFLECT

Can you recall a recent obstacle you faced? What did you learn from that experience, and how has it contributed to your personal or professional growth?

_____

_____

_____

_____

_____

_____

How do you typically react to obstacles? What mindset shifts can you make to view challenges as opportunities rather than setbacks?

_____

_____

_____

_____

_____

_____

What skills or knowledge have you gained from overcoming past obstacles? How can you apply these lessons to future challenges?

_____

_____

_____

_____

_____

_____

How do you approach problem-solving when confronted with an obstacle? What strategies can you use to enhance your problem-solving abilities and embrace the learning process?

_____

_____

_____

_____

_____

_____

In what ways can obstacles help you discover new strengths or talents that you were previously unaware of? How can you cultivate a mindset that seeks out these hidden opportunities?

_____

_____

_____

_____

_____

_____

Think of a significant obstacle you overcame in the past. How did it change your perspective or approach to similar challenges in the future?

_____

_____

_____

_____

_____

How can you create a supportive environment for yourself that encourages viewing obstacles as opportunities for growth? What resources or support systems can you tap into to help you navigate challenges more effectively?

_____

_____

_____

_____

_____

_____

DAY 5

AFFIRM

I release all fears and doubts holding me back from my true potential.

REFLECT

What specific fears or doubts have you identified that are holding you back from reaching your true potential? How do these fears manifest in your daily life?

_____

_____

_____

_____

_____

_____

Can you recall a time when you overcame a significant fear or doubt? What strategies or actions helped you move past it, and how did this impact your personal growth?

_____

_____

_____

_____

_____

_____

How do your fears and doubts affect your decision-making and actions? What steps can you take to ensure these feelings do not dictate your choices?

_____

_____

_____

_____

_____

_____

What positive affirmations or self-talk can you use to counteract your fears and doubts? How can you incorporate these into your daily routine?

_____

_____

_____

_____

_____

_____

How do you envision your life without these fears and doubts?

_____

_____

_____

_____

_____

_____

What changes would you expect to see in your personal and professional life if you released them?

_____

_____

_____

_____

_____

_____

Who in your support system can help you work through your fears and doubts? How can you involve them in your journey toward releasing these limitations?

_____

_____

_____

_____

_____

_____

What small, manageable steps can you take today to begin releasing your fears and doubts? How will you measure and celebrate your progress along the way?

_____

_____

_____

_____

_____

_____

_____

DAY 6

AFFIRM

I embrace change as a natural part of life and adapt with ease.

REFLECT

What recent changes in my life have I adapted to successfully, and what strengths did I draw upon during that process?

_____

_____

_____

_____

_____

_____

How do I typically respond to unexpected changes, and what can I do to approach them with more ease and acceptance?

_____

_____

_____

_____

_____

_____

What fears or resistance do I notice when faced with change, and how can I transform those feelings into opportunities for growth?

_____

_____

_____

_____

_____

_____

In what areas of my life am I currently resisting change, and how might embracing it lead to positive outcomes?

_____

_____

_____

_____

_____

_____

How can I better prepare myself to adapt to future changes, both emotionally and practically?

_____

_____

_____

_____

_____

_____

What role does flexibility play in my ability to embrace change, and how can I cultivate more of it in my daily life?

_____

_____

_____

_____

_____

_____

How has my perception of change evolved over time, and what have I learned about myself through the process of adaptation?

_____

_____

_____

_____

_____

_____

DAY 7

AFFIRM

I am in control of my thoughts and emotions, and I choose positivity.

REFLECT

What thoughts or emotions tend to dominate my mindset, and how can I consciously shift them toward positivity when needed?

_____

_____

_____

_____

_____

_____

_____

How do I typically react to challenging situations, and what strategies can I use to maintain a positive outlook during those times?

_____

_____

_____

_____

_____

_____

What triggers negative thoughts or emotions for me, and how can I reframe those triggers to encourage a more positive response?

_____

_____

_____

_____

_____

_____

In what ways have I successfully chosen positivity in the past, and how can I build on those experiences to strengthen my mindset?

_____

_____

_____

_____

_____

_____

How does my self-talk influence my emotions, and what steps can I take to ensure my internal dialogue supports a positive outlook?

_____

_____

_____

_____

_____

_____

What practices or habits help me stay in control of my thoughts and emotions, and how can I incorporate them more consistently into my daily life?

_____

_____

_____

_____

_____

_____

How do I balance acknowledging difficult emotions with the choice to remain positive, and what does that balance look like for me?

_____

_____

_____

_____

_____

_____

DAY 8

AFFIRM

I believe in myself and my ability to succeed against all odds.

REFLECT

What challenges or obstacles have I overcome in the past that reinforce my belief in my ability to succeed, even when the odds were against me?

_____

_____

_____

_____

_____

_____

How do I maintain confidence in myself when faced with uncertainty or adversity, and what strategies can I use to strengthen that belief?

_____

_____

_____

_____

_____

_____

What inner qualities or strengths do I possess that empower me to persevere and succeed despite difficult circumstances?

_____

_____

_____

_____

_____

_____

How do I define success in the face of adversity, and what small victories can I celebrate along the way?

_____

_____

_____

_____

_____

_____

What negative self-talk or doubts do I need to address to fully embrace my belief in my ability to succeed?

_____

_____

_____

_____

_____

_____

How can I stay motivated and focused on my goals when the path to success seems particularly challenging or unclear?

_____

_____

_____

_____

_____

_____

What role do resilience and determination play in my journey, and how can I cultivate these qualities to enhance my belief in my ability to succeed?

_____

_____

_____

_____

_____

_____

DAY 9

AFFIRM

I am worthy of achieving my goals and dreams.

REFLECT

What goals and dreams am I currently pursuing, and how do they align with my sense of purpose and self-worth?

_____

_____

_____

_____

_____

_____

What beliefs or doubts have I held about my worthiness in the past, and how can I overcome them to fully embrace my potential?

_____

_____

_____

_____

_____

_____

How do I define success for myself, and in what ways do I see myself as deserving of that success?

_____

_____

_____

_____

_____

_____

What past achievements demonstrate my ability to reach my goals, and how can I build on those successes moving forward?

_____

_____

_____

_____

_____

_____

How can I affirm my worthiness daily, and what positive self-talk or actions can reinforce my belief in my ability to achieve my dreams?

_____

_____

_____

_____

_____

_____

What external factors or influences have made me question my worthiness, and how can I shift my focus inward to trust in my own value?

_____

_____

_____

_____

_____

How do I handle setbacks or failures, and how can I use them as stepping stones rather than roadblocks on my path to achieving my goals?

_____

_____

_____

_____

_____

DAY 10

AFFIRM

I am grateful for the lessons learned from past challenges.

REFLECT

What specific challenges in my past have taught me valuable lessons, and how have those lessons shaped who I am today?

_____

_____

_____

_____

_____

_____

How do I perceive difficult experiences now compared to when I first encountered them, and what growth have I noticed in myself as a result?

_____

_____

_____

_____

_____

_____

In what ways have past challenges strengthened my resilience and ability to navigate future obstacles?

_____

_____

_____

_____

_____

_____

What lessons from past challenges have I applied to other areas of my life, and how have they contributed to my overall success or well-being?

_____

_____

_____

_____

_____

How can I express gratitude for the growth and wisdom gained from difficult experiences, even if they were painful at the time?

_____

_____

_____

_____

_____

_____

What challenges have I faced that I initially viewed as setbacks but now see as opportunities for growth?

_____

_____

_____

_____

_____

_____

How can I use the lessons learned from past challenges to support others who may be going through similar experiences?

_____

_____

_____

_____

_____

_____

DAY 11

AFFIRM

I choose to see setbacks as opportunities for growth and development.

REFLECT

What mindset shifts do you need to make to view setbacks as opportunities for growth and development rather than failures?

_____

_____

_____

_____

_____

_____

Can you identify a recent setback that you experienced? How can you reframe this experience to find the growth opportunities it presented?

_____

_____

_____

_____

_____

_____

How do you typically handle feelings of frustration or disappointment when faced with setbacks? What positive actions can you take to transform these emotions into motivation for growth?

_____

_____

_____

_____

_____

_____

What specific lessons have you learned from past setbacks, and how have these lessons contributed to your personal or professional development?

_____

_____

_____

_____

_____

_____

How can you create a plan to proactively turn future setbacks into opportunities for growth? What steps will you take to ensure you stay focused on development during challenging times?

_____

_____

_____

_____

_____

_____

What resources, support systems, or mentors can you rely on to help you see setbacks from a growth-oriented perspective? How can you strengthen these connections?

_____

_____

_____

_____

_____

_____

Reflect on a time when a setback led to unexpected positive outcomes. What did you do to turn the situation around, and how can you apply this approach to future challenges?

_____

_____

_____

_____

_____

About the Author

Vanessa R. Pittman is a New York native. When she was younger, she dreamed of becoming a writer and being financially independent. Though Vanessa was derailed from that dream, she has always been a go-getter and dedicated to her profession in radio media upon graduation from Kingsborough Community College in 1987.

Fast forward a few years later. Due to downsizing, Vanessa found herself in law enforcement, which has made her professional life extremely rewarding. Vanessa retired as a civilian from the New York City Police Department after 32 ½ years and is a 9/11 survivor.

Living as a survivor while birthing her son DeAndrè, as well as taking care of her almost one year old daughter Taélor, Vanessa had to make sure their future was secure. This meant putting her dream of being an author placed on the sidelines. As her children grew older, Vanessa needed to write down her experiences as a 9/11 survivor to deal with the trauma of that day.

Since her children have graduated from college (that is what she gets for having children back-to-back LOL), healing her mind, body, and spirit became more of an urgency. Now, 23 years later, Vanessa is still here but had to retire due to six illnesses (and counting).

While being placed on disability, she needed to realize her worth and still have time to work on things that not only benefited her, but her family as well. Vanessa realized that after such a tragic day she could survive anything once she put her mind to it. Vanessa also learned that you are never too old to learn new skills and ideas. As an empty-nester, Vanessa finally dedicated to writing this book and realize her original dream of becoming a writer.

Although she fights constant pain and depression, Vanessa is fully dedicated to telling her story and living the best life. Every day is a fight, but Vanessa will succeed and realize her goals and dreams with the time she has left. Vanesaa is extremely grateful for every day the Lord grants her regardless if it is raining, snowing, or the sun is shining. Vanessa has now realized that she has an assignment to fill to uplift others, and she plans to do it by any means necessary. Vanessa is praying this book will help others from that tragic day to find their strength and ability to navigate this burden no one asked for or saw coming.

Vanessa is married to her best friend André. They have two young adult children and reside in Laurelton, New York. She bides her time with writing her second book. Vanessa hopes to continue sharing inspiration and motivation to those around her, whether at home or on her social media.Vanessa's ultimate goal is to start a podcast and become a motivational speaker helping others heal from unresolved trauma.

www.ingramcontent.com/pod-product-compliance
Lightning Source LLC
Chambersburg PA
CBHW071152120626
46546CB00006B/2231

* 9 7 8 1 9 6 1 8 6 3 9 7 2 *